River

**Fred Chappell**

# River A Poem

LOUISIANA STATE UNIVERSITY PRESS
BATON ROUGE

ISBN 0-8071-0094-3
Library of Congress Catalog Card Number 73-91773
Copyright © 1975 by Fred Chappell
Manufactured in the United States of America

Portions of this work first appeared in *Monmouth Review*
and in *Southern Poetry Review.*

Louisiana Paperback Edition, 2000
. 09 08 07 06 05 04 03 02 01 00
5 4 3 2 1

The paper in this book meets the guidelines for permanence
and durability of the Committee on Production Guidelines
for Book Longevity of the Council on Library Resources. ♾

*To my parents*

*Let the most absent-minded of men be plunged in his deepest reveries—stand that man on his legs, set his feet a-going, and he will infallibly lead you to water, if water there be in all that region. Should you ever be athirst in the great American desert, try this experiment, if your caravan happen to be supplied with a metaphysical professor. Yes, as every one knows, meditation and water are wedded for ever.*

—Moby Dick

# Contents

# River

# I  The River Awakening in the Sea

Deep morning. Before the trees take silhouettes.

My forehead suckles your shoulder, straining to hear
In you the headlong ocean, your blood, island-saying sea now.
Wild stretches, bound to every water, of seas in you,
Uttering foam islands like broad flotillas of cabbage butterflies.
Gray tall clouds vaguely scribbling the pages of sea-top.
Your small breathing gently whetted in your nostrils, suffusing
The blood-warm pillowslip. Bedroom curls and uncurls with breath.
And all houses dark and nothing astir, though no one
Is truly asleep, everyone begins slowly to reach toward another,
Entering to each other with hands and arms impalpable, shadowless.
Slowly they turn dreaming as waves above roll deeper waves beneath.
Now they murmur amorphous words,
Words far away, no more guessable than the currents
Beginning to shudder and tremble as the hour enlarges.
Strands of current nudge into arpeggios the wide keyboards of whitebait.

                                  Perhaps now in you my body
Seeks limits, now contoured horizons
Deliver to self accustomed bitter edges.
Deliver to the man, plunging narrow in the sea, curb and margin.

Or wind diving out of the sky and raising
In the waters falling towers of lace and spittle,
Oaring underneath with strong legs so tides pile and gasp.
So corded surf comes forward half-circle,
Spreading and cataracting.

                            We are fitful in the sheets,
We clutch. My forearm digging your breast,
I am swimming your salt skin.
Early light, stringent, has opened the bedroom, searches

Crease between wall and ceiling and molds itself on the dresser
In domestic shapes: brush and comb, deodorant can, cologne bottles,
Black clots of hairpins like barbwire.
Torn sheet of light sizzles in the mirror.

Sea coming apart now, green fingers
Shaking and shredding like cobweb. The sky
Punishes the waves, in-thrusts glassy caves,
Caves growing mouthlike round spindles of wind.

Do you dream of falling?
I dream your mouth gasps numbly open, your breath caught back pulsing,
Arms outflung, protesting reckless deeps you do not escape.

How the world was formed,
The dead dropped down brick by brick to sea bottom,
The dead and the sleeping, layer upon
Layer, they hug each other forever, their bones
Grin in the fathomless dark, wary as eyes.
Here is the bedrock: the dead, fold upon fold.
Lamprotoxu, Chiasmodon,
Dragonfish, Sea Viper, Black Gulper,
Burning like comets over choked bones.

While I am wishing never to wake, the oily bull-muscle
Of sea water shoves us landward, straining and warping like kites.
Yellow ring of earth rises above burned eyes.
My senses touch daylight and recoil, the furious net
Of daylight plumbs the bed.

Continent or momentary island,
Mid-life, this land too known, too much unknown, 28 May 1971,
First day of my thirty-fifth year.
Sleeping sleeping I cannot halt the faithless instinct to be born.

The trees glow with raucous birds.
I rise and yawn,
Begin to scratch for clothing.

My naked foot upon this alien floor.

2

## II    Birthday 35: Diary Entry

1.

Multiplying my age by 2 in my head,
I'm a grandfather. Or dead.

"Midway in this life I came to a darksome wood."
But Dante, however befuddled, was Good.

And to be Good, in any viable sense,
Demands the wrought-iron primness of a Georgetown fence.

I'm still in flight, still unsteadily in pursuit,
Always becoming more sordid, pale, and acute . . .

For all the good it does . . . I'd rather seize by the neck
Some Golden Opportunity and with a mastiff shake

Empty its pockets of change;
And let my life grow bearded and strange.

In Mexico, Hunza, or Los Angeles,
I'd smoke a ton of dope and minister my fleas.

Or retiring to Monument Valley alone
With Gauguin, I'd take up saxophone.

Or slipping outside time to a Heavenly Escurial,
I'd spend a thousand years at a Monogram serial.

For though I've come so far that nothing intriguing will happen,
Like every half-assed politico I keep my options open.

My style's to veer and slide and wobble,
Immorally eavesdropping my own Babel.

When Plato divided us into Doers and Thinkers,
He didn't mean corporate generals and autoerotic bankers;

He meant that one attunes his nerves to Mind,
Or is blind.

Will may go stupid; clumsy its dance,
Mired in marmalade of circumstance.

Abjure, therefore, no ounce of alcohol.
Keep desultory and cynical.

On paper I scribble mottoes and epigrams,
Blessings and epithets, O-Holy's and Damn's—

Not matter sufficient to guard a week by.
The wisdom I hoard you could stuff in your eye.

But *everything* means *something,* that's my faith;
Despair begins when they stop my mouth.

Drunk as St. Francis I preach to the cat.
I even talk back to the TV set.

Sometimes I even Inquisition my wife:
"Susan, *is* there a moral alternative to life?"

Partly because I want to know, partly because
I'm amused by sleazy cleverness.

I can talk till the moon dissolves, till the stars
Splash down in the filth of morning newspapers.

Talk that engenders a fearful itch
Always just barely not quite out of reach.

Talk with purposes so huge and vague,
The minor details are Om and Egg.

Surely something gets said if only in intent,
When the magnesium candle of enthusiasm is burnt.

Happy Birthday to me! At age thirty-five
I scratch to see if I'm yet alive.

Thumbing the ledger of thirty-five years,
I find unstartled I'm badly in arrears.

In fact, I'm up to my eyes in debt
Unpayable. And not done suffering yet.

But then, so what?
What you think you owe is everything you're not.

That's not true debt, but merely guilt,
Irrelevant though heartfelt;

Merely part of the noisy lovers' quarrel
We name Doctrine, Dialectic, and Moral.

I'd sleep in the eiderdown of the True Believer
And never nightmare about Either/Or

If I had a different person in my head.
But this gnawing worm shows that I'm not dead.

Therefore: either I live with doubt
Or get out.

2.

(While I ponder and point this offhand apologia
for a life I find ungainly and sinister as
a black umbrella, my gaze settles and unsettles
in the bourgeois landscape outside the window where:
a row of day lilies gives a livid razzberry to
the beige terrier peeing against our dented
garbage can with all the complacent unconcern
of a Polish steelworker who once went four
bloody rounds with Carmen Basilio and by
God doesn't care who knows it.
                                                    If I
could choose I'd be the sunlight which comes
down like melting butter, dripping in white
spots the flanks of things and carbonating the

dog's not-quite-tan stiff hairs one by one.
*That* is a mode of being, just but not
fatuous, which one aches for but cannot
—without madness—strive toward, alas.

Do dogs keep diaries? Do lilies?

They should.)

3.

I'd like to believe anything is possible.
That I could walk out on a midnight full

Of stars and hear an omniscient Voice say,
"Well, Fred, for a change you had a good day.

You didn't do anything so terribly awful.
Even your thoughts were mostly lawful.

I'm pleased." —Or that by accident I'd find
A tablet headed, *Carry this message to mankind.*

—Or that simply by dreaming I'd find out
What subnuclear physics is all about.

But nothing like that is in the cards.
Bit by scroungy bit knowledge affords

Itself; and what the angels know, or don't,
My brain would reduce absolutely to cant.

Wherefore, my soul, be thou content.
"Man, I'd love to, but I *ain't*."

Why not? Each time I reach outside my skin,
I just get lonesome for what's within.

I know the future I will not trust,
And here in the present as an overnight guest

At the Holiday Inn of Crooked Dream
I nurse the one-eyed flame

Of bitter regret
And shriek "You bastards haven't got me yet!"

At phantoms who know damn well they have,
Now and to the hour of the grave.

Whatever they say, Time's not a river;
It is a slow harsh fever

Of things trying not to go smash,
A wilderness of wind and ash.

When I went to the river I saw willows
Splashing down, oil-slick of pinks and yellows

And purples, and leaning over the edge of grass
I saw, darkened, my own face.

On the bank of Time I saw nothing human,
No man, no woman,

No animals or plants; only moon
Upon moon, sterile stone

Climbing the steep hill of void.
And I was afraid.

Please, Lord. I want to go to some forever
Where water is, and live there.

I want a sky that rain drops from,
Soothing the intemperate loam;

An eternity where a man can buy a drink
For a buddy, or a good-looking chick.

If there's no hereafter with hot and cold running
I'm simply not coming.

Not that I doubt Your willingness to provide,
But, Lord, You stand on one side

Of the infinite black ditch
And I on the other. *And that's a bitch.*

But I'm going to take it for granted
That honey Elysium is plentifully planted

With trout streams and waterfalls and suburban
Swimming pools, and sufficient chaser for bourbon.

Lead me then, Lord, to the thundering valleys where
Cool silver droplets feather the air;

Where rain like thimbles smacks roofs of tin,
Washing away sin;

Where daily a vast and wholesome cloud
Announces itself aloud.

                              Amen.

## III    My Grandmother Washes Her Feet

I see her still, unsteadily riding the edge
Of the clawfoot tub, mumbling to her feet,
Musing bloodrust water about her ankles.
Cotton skirt pulled up, displaying bony
Bruised patchy calves that would make you weep.

Rinds of her soles had darkened, crust-colored—
Not yellow now—like the tough outer belly
Of an adder. In fourteen hours the most refreshment
She'd given herself was dabbling her feet in the water.

"You mightn't've liked John-Giles. Everybody knew
He was a mean one, galloping whiskey and bad women
All night. Tried to testify dead drunk
In church one time. That was a ruckus. Later
Came back a War Hero, and all the young men
Took to doing the things he did. And failed.
Finally one of his women's men shot him."

"What for?"

                    "Stealing milk through fences . . . . That part
Of Family nobody wants to speak of.
They'd rather talk about fine men, brick houses,
Money. Maybe you ought to know, teach you
Something."

                    "What *do* they talk about?"

                                        "Generals,
And the damn Civil War, and marriages.
Things you brag about in the front of Bibles.

You'd think there was arms and legs of Family
On every battlefield from Chickamauga
To Atlanta."

       "That's not the way it is?"

"Don't matter how it is. No proper way
To talk, is all. It was nothing they ever did.
And plenty they *won't* talk about . . . John-Giles!"

Her cracked toes thumped the tub wall, spreading
Shocklets. Amber toenails curled like shavings.
She twisted the worn knob to pour in coolness
I felt suffuse her body like a whiskey.

"Bubba Martin, he was another, and no
Kind of man. Jackleg preacher with the brains
Of a toad. Read the Bible upsidedown and crazy
Till it drove him crazy, making crazy marks
On doorsills, windows, sides of Luther's barn.
He killed hisself at last with a shotgun.
No gratitude for Luther putting him up
All those years. Shot so he'd fall down the well."

"I never heard."

       "They never mention him.
Nor Aunt Annie, that everybody called
Paregoric Annie, that roamed the highways
Thumbing cars and begging change to keep
Even with her craving. She claimed she was saving up
To buy a glass eye. It finally shamed them
Enough, they went together and got her one.
That didn't stop her. She lugged it around
In a velvet-lined case, asking strangers
Please to drop it in the socket for her.
They had her put away. And that was that.
There's places Family ties just won't stretch to."

Born then in my mind a race of beings
Unknown and monstrous. I named them Shadow-Cousins,
A linked long dark line of them,
Peering from mirrors and gleaming in closets, agog
To manifest themselves inside myself.
Like discovering a father's cancer.
I wanted to search my body for telltale streaks.

"Sounds like a bunch of cow thieves."

                                        "Those too, I reckon,
But they're forgotten or covered over so well
Not even I can make them out. Gets foggy
When folks decide they're coming on respectable.
First thing you know, you'll have a Family Tree."

(I imagined a wind-stunted horse-apple.)

She raised her face. The moons of the naked bulb
Flared in her spectacles, painting out her eyes.
In dirty water light bobbed like round soap.
A countenance matter-of-fact, age-engraved,
Mulling in peaceful wonder petty annals
Of embarrassment. Gray but edged with brown
Like an old photograph, her hair shone yellow.
A tiredness mantled her fine energy.
She shifted, sluicing water under instep.

"O what's the use," she said. "Water seeks
Its level. If your daddy thinks that teaching school
In a white shirt makes him a likelier man,
What's to blame? Leastways, he won't smother
Of mule-farts or have to starve for a pinch of rainfall.
Nothing new gets started without the old's
Plowed under, or halfway under. We sprouted from dirt,
Though, and it's with you, and dirt you'll never forget."

"No Mam."

"Don't you say me No Mam yet.
Wait till you get your chance to deny it."

Once she giggled, a sound like stroking muslin.

"You're bookish. I can see you easy a lawyer
Or a county clerk in a big white suit and tie,
Feeding the preacher and bribing the sheriff and the judge.
Second-generation-respectable
Don't come to any better destiny.
But it's dirt you rose from, dirt you'll bury in.
Just about the time you'll think your blood
Is clean, here will come dirt in a natural shape
You never dreamed. It'll rise up saying, Fred,
Where's that mule you're supposed to march behind?
Where's your overalls and roll-your-owns?
Where's your Blue Tick hounds and Domineckers?
Not all the money in this world can wash true-poor
True rich. Fatback just won't change to artichokes."

"What's artichokes?"

                          "Pray Jesus you'll never know.
For if you do it'll be a sign you've grown
Away from what you are, can fly to flinders
Like a touch-me-not . . . I may have errored
When I said *true-poor*. It ain't the same
As dirt-poor. When you got true dirt you got
Everything you need . . . And don't you say me
Yes Mam again. You just wait."

                          She leaned
And pulled the plug. The water circled gagging
To a bloody eye and poured in the hole like a rat.
I thought maybe their spirits had gathered there,
All my Shadow-Cousins clouding the water,
And now they ran to earth and would cloud the earth.
Effigies of soil, I could seek them out

By clasping soil, forcing warm rude fingers
Into ancestral jelly my father wouldn't plow.
I strained to follow them, and never did.
I never had the grit to stir those guts.
I never had the guts to stir that earth.

## IV  Cleaning the Well

Two worlds there are. One you think
You know; the Other is the Well.
In hard December down I went.
"Now clean it out good." Lord, I sank
Like an anchor. My grand-dad leant
Above. His face blazed bright as steel.

Two worlds, I tell you. Swallowed by stones
Adrip with sweat, I spun on the ache
Of the rope; the pulley shrieked like bones
Scraped merciless on violins.
Plunging an eye. Plunging a lake
Of corkscrew vertigo and silence.

I halfway knew the rope would break.

Two suns I entered. At exact noon
The white sun narrowly hung above;
Below, like an acid floating moon,
The sun of water shone.
And what beneath that? A monster trove

Of blinding treasure I imagined:
Ribcage of drowned warlock gleaming,
Rust-chewed chain mail, or a plangent
Sunken bell tolling to the heart
Of earth. (They'd surely chosen an art-
less child to sound this soundless dreaming

O.) Dropping like a meteor,
I cried aloud—"Whoo! It's *God
Damn* cold!"—dancing the skin of the star.

"You watch your mouth, young man," he said.
I jerked and cursed in a silver fire
Of cold. My left leg thrummed like a wire.

Then, numb. Well water rose to my waist
And I became a figure of glass,
A naked explorer of outer space.
Felt I'd fricasseed my ass.
Felt I could stalk through earth and stone,
Nerveless creature without a bone.

Water-sun shattered, jelly-
bright wavelets lapped the walls.
Whatever was here to find, I stood
In the lonesome icy belly
Of the darkest vowel, lacking breath and balls,
Brain gummed mud.

"Say, Fred, how's it going down there?"
His words like gunshots roared; re-roared.
I answered, "Well—" (*Well well well . . .* )
And gave it up. It goes like Hell,
I thought. Precise accord
Of pain, disgust, and fear.

"Clean it out good." He drifted pan
And dipper down. I knelt and dredged
The well floor. Ice-razors edged
My eyes, the blackness flamed like fever,
Tin became nerve in my hand
Bodiless. *I shall arise never.*

What did I find under this black sun?
Twelve plastic pearls, monopoly
Money, a greenish rotten cat,
Rubber knife, toy gun,

Clock guts, wish book, door key,
An indescribable female hat.

Was it worth the trip, was it true Descent?
Plumbing my childhood, to fall
Through the hole in the world and become . . .
What? *He told me to go. I went.*
(Recalling something beyond recall.
Cold cock on the nether roof of Home.)

Slouch sun swayed like a drunk
As up he hauled me, up, up,
Most willing fish that was ever caught.
I quivered galvanic in the taut
Loop, wobbled on the solid lip
Of earth, scarcely believing my luck.

His ordinary world too rich
For me, too sudden. Frozen blue,
Dead to armpit, I could not keep
My feet. I shut my eyes to fetch
Back holy dark. Now I knew
All my life uneasy sleep.

Jonah, Joseph, Lazarus,
Were you delivered so? Ript untimely
From black wellspring of death, unseemly
Haste of flesh dragged forth?
Artemis of waters, succor us,
Oversurfeit with our earth.

My vision of light trembled like steam.
I could not think. My senses drowned
In Arctic Ocean, the Pleiades
Streaked in my head like silver fleas.
I could not say what I had found.
I cannot say my dream.

When life began re-tickling my skin
My bones shuddered me. Sun now stood
At one o'clock. Yellow. Thin.
*I had not found death good.*
"Down there I kept thinking I was dead."

"Aw, you're all right," he said.

## V   Susan Bathing

> Here Earth and Water seem to strive again,
> Not *Chaos*-like together crush'd and bruis'd,
> But as the World, harmoniously confus'd.

> —Alexander Pope
> *Windsor Forest*

You
are rejoicement, fair flesh erect in the porcelain & the
bee-eyed steel showerhead ogling & touching you and
I would make a Renaissance poet's wish, to be the pleasing
showerhead touching you with a hundred streaming fingers
wandering so close your body completely to your feet, or
I wish to be the worn white tub you stand in, would
be like a snowy garden with a single grand delicate flower
or a fountain which receives or maybe a statue which was never
shaped nor even dreamed of but nevertheless was born in and from
earth of antiquity, exhumed time past standing wet to haunt time
present & to encroach now upon sleeping and waking, every moment
to darken and illumine at once like the picnic ground in the oak
grove when June wind sifts like a dropped poker
deck the deep green leaves above, fluttery tide of them untying
itself upon a breaker of breeze, and you & I beneath swing between
us the wicker basket & wool army blanket, coming to the shade wary
for acrid horsenettle and dried buggy cowflop, because this is how I
pray we shall together die, coming forward to the shade hand in hand,
alert & neither happy nor grieving & our spirits together as close as
at this moment upon your flushed skin the soapy warm hand of water is
spread and slides, for a second pausing about your feet & then drifting
to the dark naught of the drain and going away, just as many times
in dreams I have sweated to chase some quick gleam of you instantly
unrecognized & then too eagerly leaped at, & then it darted gone
forever through a silent hole in my mind like childhood dragon

flies I pursued iridescent in sunlight & precious but in the shadow under
Beaverdam Creek Bridge invisible, uncatchable, becoming creatures only
of remorseful imagination, but these dreamed partial ghosts now obliterate
as now I see all your naked animal moving under drumming
water, strong neck grown taut & misty droplets smudge your chin
and as you scrub the azure cloth on your left shoulder the right elbow
thrusts out of plane, obtruding the perfect distance between us & therefore
has made claim, living and tactile and feeling, upon my own space of
breathing & feeling, upon my responsibilities to whatever is genuine, for you
are I know actual, actual and urgent as starvation and all other
rational disasters & botches of mortality, more actual
than these because your reddened elbow pokes forward into time
present iterating that beauty too is Jesus! urgent (*O what shall
I do with my hands & paunch? shall I hide my eyes? my face
in my hands blots to a mush like a rotten canteloupe*), that
unattending beauty is danger & mortal sin, and that no matter how my
heart is abashed & my senses quaked in the viscera, I
must cleave to speech, speech being my single knowledge, speech-praise,
though this speech clings only a soiled atomic
instant about your bare feet before pouring fast to the black
mouth of the pipe to smother in dirt and stone, yet why
should you not accept my words as water for water also would
be praise freely burgeoning out of air and friendly upon the skin
to gladden nerve-ends so the pores shall open & sing unsounding
like baby swallows when the mother darts quick out of open
air, ordinary as a summer shower, bringing lunch, this if only
once I could know surely you opened to praise, unfolded unthinking
like a cold hand brought to the campfire, and why not *why not*
saying of praise as instrument of unclosing and rising toward light
& free water, for if not praiseful speech the spirit is stopped off
in the throat where the clavicles come near to join before the body
begins to fever & tremble frustrate like a grenade which was aching
& aching to devour itself in a fountain of light & surprise, and
do not halt it, for once the mind prepares to praise & garbs
in worshipful robe it enlarges to plenitude, vastness of names

qualities numbers and points of kinship, and a criminal cheap
death ensues if it cannot utter, as my mouth utters water having
now become the stainless showerhead to search you with a hundred
tongues, slope and shadow of you, hollow of your shoulder where
dim soapfleece lingers & the eyelid-shaped shadows beneath your
breasts & strands of shining bone at wrists silvery as trout bellies
& loose fingerlings of hair damp-curling beside the ear & on your
pink flanks water a moment holding in little beads like dew on
the bedroom window with new sun behind & shining through as your skin
in this water flames & small of your back gently curving so the drops
collect in a transparent pendant delta & the crisp fleece before sequined
and thrilling with drops like a G-string in white bare light turned
on after all the sailors are hauled away drunk rubbing palms across
bleeding lips, & in this spangled fleece is a singular water also
praise, speech-praise spoken from necessity & to keep alive praise
in the sweet creatures in their cores & the smooth thighs veiny
with water errant and trackless though discoverable always discoverable
in clarity, thigh slightly shuddering at the cool accidental touch
of wall tile & then toward my mouth saying all this in water you raise
& open your mouth and I enter in & am warm in tongue and throat until
through praise I begin to suffuse all through you and even to emerge
all about you a radiance shining like silver leaf smeared around a
pensive joyous Tuscan madonna seeing Latin tumble backward out of
the annunciation angel's mouth and who has not quite opened yet her
mouth to receive the news pouring forward, news which also is praise
of woman, Ave, plena gratia, Woman thou shalt with thy flesh utter
living one word origin and end of praise forever, praise to suffer
violate inviolable amid black shame and stony unknowing of those
who grudge hate maim & murder & finally deafen themselves to even
the great waters all day and night traversing the heavens & under whose
shadows they harm & kill, ignorant that shade of water is light, that death
shall be method of praise under a sky which rains the light &
water mingled together from which our unenviable brotherhood arose, light
and water cleaving together as this too-cool bathroom light mixes drily
burning with each water-bead to form now you, Susan, as you that clean

space hold & compose as at once you burst it, jamming the whole
a thoughtful palpable object upon my flickering senses so that an
object impersonal also intimate as a touch at groin you are, as if
*Clementia* on heavy vellum page caught fire & scorched the tracks from my
finger ends & the nails melted & sparse hairs on my forearms flared
up, as if at the foot of my bed at midnight appeared a Sphinx of timeless
water gazing upon' me with pity too huge to say, bewailing me because
no word is so expressive as water which in her being she articulates & I
senseless & too broken to know and cannot advance to praise, my
mouth unhinged swinging idiot slack like the door of a ruined barn the wind
molests & my eyes filmed over with thick oils of self-pride, my skin
anesthetized deadly, so that in darkest waters of sleeping I move
unyielding to water, stolid mud mountain water enfolds & does not
enlighten, stockstill in my thought as if God had never said *Let there
be,* scissoring the firmaments, & the Sphinx of water shapes now Herself
to a single tear reflecting my chest & face elongate, scared by salt vision
of self-ignorance, seeing myself in bitter water stretched out in death
white & wavering wraithlike in a mirror containing me but which I cannot
touch, but here a clarifying suspicion approaches, that the Sphinx is
yourself, Susan, then when you wring rinsing the azure cloth at your waist,
upper arms at your ribs, your form now retreat into flattened space
suggesting eternity, only faintly human at this moment, outline
human as in Byzantine mosaics, but an obscuring water stands between us,
pallid cloud of steam shrugging upward its shoulders & its pearl
torso swelling forward maybe in threat but certainly your solid volume
veiled, so I must plead, Why do you go away? where do you go? will you
again return from behind the spiritual mists & acquaint again
my senses? or are you for good ascended into ideal spaces & rely upon
my hurt memory to limn your shape my heart starves to join, do not
so scar my will I plead you, for my will is stricken and contort,
its own most effort has fouled & burst it & only intercession from
without can restore it, and so I see grateful at last the toilet cistern
begin to sweat, the panes of the narrow window run in streaks, the mirror
show patches of white room with angles clear & strait, and thank God your
body! too reappears pink-glowing and spread about it its own scent,

washed skin renewed like a grand delicate flower rebloomed, and your
face I see lilylike shining light as porcelain beneath water shining
light, eyes dark but accustomed to this white light and intelligent
of form in all spaces & modes whatsoever, AND adoration in the wet
air coalesces, I can & will believe that hymns are sung and cherubim
puffing out their cheeks like chipmunks strew the gray linoleum with
evanescent flowers that touch & melt, snowflakes of flowers unique
& instantly mortal returned to soil of water, ubiquitous surface
reaching from this closed air and clasping, painting each sleek plane
as masseurs rubbed down the lion-colored wrestlers with oil so
they would appear immune to grasp, so that entrance to the space
Ajax collected insured not at all hand should find his lithe & strong
limbs and hold, in this manner you are seen, gauzy curtains of steam
drop away and all ablush and damp, tea-rose dew-drowned, you stand
a moment pensive before lifting the dun rough terry towel & loosing it,
folds disclosing in silent slow movement like a film warped almost
to timelessness, your flesh more fleshly-seeming because the cloth
opposes it in texture, and with it begin to swaddle your body, tugging &
twisting in its snug cocoon, and how will you now this chrysalis
exit, all over rubbed warm & smiling at last as if you dreamed
this very second you were not here, your body remaining yet sailed
away on streams of atoms into the winds and is sweetening now zephyrs
by Bermuda & Mykonos or gustily invading the spicy Virgins, it would be true
since I could I do believe your spirit has power in air, the same
dominion strong over land & sea that wind & water cherish, unspotted freedom
intact proud fierce if it come to point but happy & clear by nature and
by nature selfless of its own character as the dropping rivulet on
Fires Creek Mountain that fed & fed the moss-painted stone we saw, stone
greenly avid for water it can never digest and which again relooped
below sliding rot-black log & snaking under mirk humus & stone jumble
till we had mostly fallen the steep trail and saw this water quiet
& widen to a stream hand-broad final, its destination sure
to Little Fires where dark laurels hang over & black gnats swarm
in big funnel shapes & the rainbows lie still at boiling pool heads &
gurgle among rocks makes above the stream an elegant baroque

fountain of sound varying shapely refreshing as canon for clavier,
for I know it would be your nature to drift into the serious currents
of earth & sky, to nudge until absorbed by root & tendril, assuage
compassionately amative hungers, and so wherever you are you are
here too rubbing your left shin rested on the toilet seat so deliberately
you might be polishing marble, half-hypnotized by the pleasurable
warm abrading, knowing perhaps a distance obtains although your hand
moves on your pale leg, a distance between them obtains and though
touching they shall never meet, distance obtaining as between mouth
& word mouth forms, speech praise, fire carried up in a cave missing
its roof yet brightness reaches from the mouth outwards and is
known by who cares to see & hear, lighting what wishes to be lit, thus
you polish yourself as Catullus with pumice eternally scraped
from his word the verdigris and this is after all, Lady, what you are,
a word, maybe like Woodstar the name of a hummingbird or maybe
from books a classy Latin name for a flower Ipomoea purpurea dark
pink Morning Glory with a burst black star at center, bell of this
trumpet holding in one drop of early water the sun burning yellow
and drowned in that globe, plenum of dew, and if we march to fields
to see the universe made bitsy in the flower we shall feel about us
water-presence water-immanence though the sky be blue scoured
silk, a clear day & no hint of rain & mists blown away, yet
we shall feel at the backs of our necks water unstoppable in
arteries of grass vines and even the mica-flecked gray
stones inhabited by invisibly attenuate fogs of water as houses
hold always webbed glimmers, presence of families who have died
within, and so rub as you will upon the poem you are, the word
still shall be muscular with water-impulse, informing every tendon
& nerve & your way of seeing, it has come down to you from
grandmothers grandfathers mother & father, it is inescapable as time
when you twist the sinewed towel about you muffling your clean
flesh the synonym of love, somewhat muffling but not eradicating,
for in your face & eyes & hands it sings clear, and do you understand how
it is praise, love is praise, Susan, of what is, and if it be prisoned
in low earth it shall bound in high air saying like howitzers its

name and if it be scurried to & fro over cold wastes of skies yet
shall it touch with all its names blade root stone roof and if
it be locked solid at both poles there it shall say its name with
infinite unthinking purity, where it is hardest for men to live
with and even so they wrest its substance there and men there are
gentlest of any peoples where animals too go robed churchly in
white, nowhere would you escape it, for dark of night flooding on
is water and when you sleep those are strong cables of water towing
you slack through all the names you might say or take and when
you move sportive or lovemaking it is water which faucets jet & direct
flashing and when you regard children it is water becoming a warm
osmotic cell surrounded by water, and death too is a drowsing black
unmoving lake below the throats of all springs & founts whatsoever
where they draw bright energies and can gleam in the woods like
foamflowers, but you have already known water is not to fear, and
now when you take my hand absentmindedly in your cool hand I feel
bathed also, I feel washed quite brilliant, I feel rising helpless
to my mouth your name   Susan Susan   and now I do say it in praise of
you.

## VI    Dead Soldiers

I remember seven floods, the worst
In 1946 when the sluice-gates burst
And logs came blundering from the paper mill,
Choking Pigeon River below Smathers Hill,
Clanging culvert pipes and headfirst fast
Into Fiberville Bridge. It wouldn't last,
Old lattice-work of peeling paint and rust.
Everyone gathered at Campbell's store just
To see how long before it broke.
                              Old man
Campbell was unabashedly drunk again.
(Not that he hadn't good cause—this time, at least.)
His house and store stood the flood-bank, yellow yeast
And black poison water already chewing
Off his lower lawn. Five big logs slewing
Down kidnapped his pumphouse. He swore in angry
Disbelief when he saw it strew in the hungry
Acids. "Sweet Jesus Christamighty Gawd,"
He said, and spat whiskey spittle at the broad
And broadening river. "Somebody ought to by Christ
*Do* something. A man could stand it oncet . . . but *twicet*—"

No one offering to halt the flood, he took
A drink and held his pint to the light to look
How much. Three-quarters gone. He swigged it off
One gulp, turned purple, and began to cough.
"Somebody by God ought—"

                              The only help
He got was thumping on his back for a gulp
Of desperate breath. He dropped the empty, staring

Morose at piebald pine and oak logs boring
Chopped butts a moment up into drizzly day
Light, dipping like porpoises, swooping away
Toward Tennessee. "Guy works and slaves and where's
It get you," he said. "A limp dick, gray hairs,
A pile of debt is all I know. You'd think
The goddam Mill would've thought—"

                                  Midnight ink
Ineradicable, the flood kept swelling, blacking the rose
Garden laid back out of elm-reach where snows
Could quilt it warm. "If Elsie was alive she'd die
To see it." Dime-sized rain from the sagging sky
Dropped and he raised his startled face. *"Son
Of a bitch."* The farmers gaping him for fun
Began to mumble, thinking how more rain
Would ruin them too. If it happened again—
Having been flooded two years before—they'd have
Bank notes so deep only a Peace Valley grave
Could free them.

                Suddenly Campbell departed the hill,
Dashed into his house, and returned ready to kill
Somebody or maybe only something, bearing
New whiskey, a .22 rifle, shells; and swearing
Rare enough to shame a rattlesnake.
Instantly he gained respect.

                        "Chrisake,
Virgil, what you doing?"

                        "I ain't going to stand
Here and not fight back what's taking my land
And house," he said.

                    "You can't goddammit shoot
A river."

              He spat. "I'd like to know why not."

And so he did. Loaded, and started pumping
Slug after slug at the water rising and thumping
His house like a big bass drum. All at once
The basement doors burst open and out floated tons,
Or what seemed tons, of emptied whiskey jars.

"Lord, Virgil, did you drink all that?"

                          "Sure's
You're damned I did." He grinned. "But the goddam dead
Soldiers won't stay dead. Must be," he said,
"The goddam Day of Resurrection." And started in
Picking them off. Insensible husks of gin,
Bourbon, scotch, and moonshine sank as once more
He killed them certain. How many? At least a score
Of each, though nobody counted, struck dumb no doubt
At load on load of bottles rumbling out.
He never missed. He must have known by heart
Where each one sat on the shelf. Maybe a part
Of his crazy pride was knowing to a decimal point
How much he drank, having little to flaunt
Himself with else. Or maybe this unguessed cache
Of glassware was to him not splendid trash
But secret treasure he alone knew how
To value, now bobbing away in the fearful flow.
Anyway, he shot them to splinters, accurate
As cancer, muttering no one could quite hear what.
At last he busted them all. At last they'd never
Rise again, bright jewels in pitch river.

And now we heard a great inanimate groan,
A scream of something dying that stretched bone
And muscle in electric spasm. Enormous shriek
Of shearing iron made our knees go weak.
The bridge was falling. Drooping in curlicues
Like licorice, and shrugging up torn spews
Of shouting metal, and widening outward like a mouth

Slowly grinning to show each snagged-off tooth,
It plunged the water with a noise like the fall of Rome.
Everyone hollered at once. Gray boil of foam
And halved girders jumped cloudward between the piers,
Subsiding in a hail of bolts.

                    No cheers
Then, no laughing, but a silence solemn and deep
As church spread in the crowd like opiate half-sleep.
The great event was over; they'd finally seen
It all. A post-coital calm flushed clean
Their senses as they turned bright-glazed eyes
Toward mired roads home under purpling pink-streaked skies.

That's what I think *they* saw. But what *I* saw
Was Virgil Campbell with a meaningful slow
Smile lift his gun, and just when the bridge tumbled
He fired upon it a single shot, and grumbled,
"Better put it out of its misery."

After twenty-five murky years I still see
Him there, crazed Minuteman at river edge
With a .22 Marlin bringing down a bridge.

                              *

*"Well, here you are at last," my father said.*
*"I've been looking for you." I turned my head*
*To find him suddenly solid in sudden dusk*
*Behind me, shape looming lightless, and gravid musk*
*Of cigarettes and wet wool standing like smoke*
*About him, an imminent immuring cloak*
*Formless. But awesome as God to a child of ten.*
*"Don't tell me you've got so dumb you don't know when*
*It's milking time." I followed him to the truck*
*And we went wallowing home through rutted muck.*
*"Virgil Campbell took a .22*
*And shot the iron bridge down," I said.*

*"That's true,"*
*He said presently, "if you think so. I can*
*Swear to it he's an independent man."*

*And nothing else for a while. At the barn he*
*Added, "That must have been something to see."*

# VII    My Grandfather Gets Doused

He hedged his final bet.
The old man decided, to get saved
You had to get *all* wet.

An early April Sunday he braved
Cold river and a plague
Of cold Baptist stares. He waved

And nodded. I saw his wounded leg
Wince at the touch
Of icy stream-edge.

Righteous clutch
Of the preacher dragged him farther in.
Maybe now he didn't want it much,

But ringed by mutely sniggering men
And contraltos making moues,
He managed a foolish unaccustomed grin

And plunged to his knees in ooze
And rush of Pigeon River.
What a bad black bruise

Of reputation! Never
In a thousand thousand thousand years
Had Davis or Clark turned hard-believer

Baptist. Weeping wormy tears
His Methodist fathers screamed
In paid-for plots. My uncles' sneers

Rose like spiritual kites. Who dreamed
Heresy lurked in his slick Sibelius-like head?
It was not seemly what he seemed.

Dead,
And grounded like a hog or horsefly, would
Be better than raving Baptist. No one admitted

It, but to be good
Was to be Methodist.
*And everybody should.*

Man, were they ever pissed!
He'd taken the habit of laying down laws,
So now this exhibitionist

Apostasy didn't sit so well.
And they all felt sneaky-content because
There went *his* ass to hell.

They'd togged him out in white,
And he rose from the water with a look
As naked and contrite

As a fifth-grader caught with a dirty book.
*Was he truly saved at last?*
Before he could take it back

They said the words fast
And hustled him to dry ground
And shook his hand with ungracious haste.

If his theology was unsound,
At least he had a healthy fear
Of dying . . . . He frowned

When he saw me gaping. A double tear
Bloomed at the rim of his eye.
In a yellow-green willow a finch sang clear

And high.
Silence seized us every one,
Standing bemused and dry.

Now O pitiful he looked. The sun
Cloud-muffled, a cold wind-stir
Brought us to compassion.

They fetched his clothes from the car;
Still expostulating,
The preacher led him to a laurel thicket where

He changed. *And changed again.* Waiting
In numb wonder, we heard his voice go
Grating.

Baptized he was. But now
He decided to be *un*baptized. Pale
Pale the preacher grew;

I thought his heart would fail.
"No, Mr. Davis, no no no." It couldn't be.
Baptism was all or not at all,

Like virginity.
He'd have to stay washed white,
Baptist through eternity.

"Well, that's all right,"
He said. "But I had no notion it *took* so quick."
His voice glared unworldly light.

Grasped his walking stick,
And saddling his armpit on his crutch, he strode,
Dragging the dead foot like a brick.

At the side of the narrow road
He turned to watch the river driving east.
(Was West Fork Pigeon *really* the Blood

Of the Lamb?) A shadow-creased
Scowl huddled his face
When a thought bubbled up like yeast:

The water that saved him was some place
Else now, washing away the sins
Of trout down past McKinnon Trace.

And now he hoisted his stoic limbs
Into the home-bound Ford. "What damn difference
Will it make?" he said. "Sometimes
I think I ain't got a lick of sense."

## VIII  My Grandmother Washes Her Vessels

In the white-washed medical-smelling milkhouse
She wrestled clanging steel; grumbled and trembled,
Hoisting the twenty-gallon cans to the ledge
Of the spring-run (six by three, a concrete grave
Of slow water). Before she toppled them in—
Dented armored soldiers booming in pain—
She stopped to rest, brushing a streak of damp
Hair back, white as underbark. She sighed.

"I ain't strong enough no more to heft these things.
I could now and then wish for a man
Or two . . . Or maybe not. More trouble, likely,
Than what their rations will get them to do."

The August six-o'clock sunlight struck a wry
Oblong on the north wall. Yellow light entering
This bone-white milkhouse recharged itself white,
Seeped pristine into the dozen strainer cloths
Drying overhead.

                    "Don't you like men?"

Her hand hid the corner of her childlike grin
Where she'd dropped her upper plate and left a gap.
"Depends on the use you want them for," she said.
"Some things they're good at, some they oughtn't touch."

"Wasn't Grandaddy a good carpenter?"

She nodded absentminded. "He was fine.
Built churches, houses, barns in seven counties.
Built the old trout hatchery on Balsam . . .
Here. Give me a hand."

                              We lifted down
Gently a can and held it till it drowned.
Gushed out of its headless neck a musky clabber
Whitening water like a bedsheet ghost.
I thought, Here spills the soldier's spirit out;
If I could drink a sip I'd know excitements
He has known; travails, battles, tourneys,
A short life fluttering with pennants.

                                   She grabbed
A frazzly long-handled brush and scrubbed his innards
Out. Dun flakes of dried milk floated up,
Streamed drainward. In his trachea water sucked
Obscenely, graying like a storm-sky.

"You never told me how you met."

                                   She straightened,
Rubbed the base of her spine with a dripping hand.
"Can't recollect. Some things, you know, just seem
To go clear from your mind. Probably
He spotted me at prayer meeting, or it could
Have been a barn-raising. That was the way
We did things then. Not like now, with the men
All hours cavorting up and down in cars."

Again she smiled. I might have sworn she winked.

"But what do you remember?"

                              "Oh, lots of things.
About all an old woman is good for
Is remembering . . . . But getting married to Frank
Wasn't the beginning of my life.
I'd taught school up Greasy Branch since I
Was seventeen. And I took the first census
Ever in Madison County. You can't see
It now, but there was a flock of young men come

Knocking on my door. If I'd a mind
I could have danced six nights of the week."

We tugged the cleaned can out, upended it
To dry on the worn oak ledge, and pushed the other
Belching in. Slowly it filled and sank.

"Of course, it wasn't hard to pick Frank out,
The straightest-standing man I ever saw.
Had a waxed moustache and a chestnut mare.
Before I'd give my say I made him cut
That moustache off. I didn't relish kissing
A briar patch. He laughed when I said that,
Went home and shaved . . . . It wasn't the picking and saying
That caused me ponder, though. Getting married—
In church—in front of people—for good and all:
It makes you pause. Here I was twenty-eight,
Strong and healthy, not one day sick since I
Was born. What cause would I have to be waiting
On a man?"

                    Suddenly she sat on the spring-run edge
And stared bewildered at empty air, murmuring.

"I never said this to a soul, I don't
Know why . . . I told my papa, 'Please hitch me
The buggy Sunday noon. I can drive
Myself to my own wedding.' That's what I did,
I drove myself. A clear June day as cool
As April, and I came to where we used to ford
Laurel River a little above Coleman's mill,
And I stopped the horse and I thought and thought.
*If I cross this river I won't turn back.* I'll join
To that blue-eyed man as long as I've got breath.
There won't be nothing I can feel alone
About again. My heart came to my throat.
I suppose I must have wept. And then I heard

36

A yellowhammer in a willow tree
Just singing out, ringing like a dance-fiddle
Over the gurgly river-sound, just singing
To make the whole world hush to listen to him.
And then my tears stopped dropping down, and I touched
Nellie with the whip, and we crossed over."

# IX  Science Fiction Water Letter to Guy Lillian

May 28, 1971

Dear Guy,

It
is not quite true I said science fiction images
lack imagination. What they lack is resonance.
The usual s-f novel is as numb, deaf, and
odorless as a patient readied for surgery.
Surely imagination is sensual, truthfully
septic, like a child wallowing his dog. S-f is
self-indulgent also, but less pleasurable to
the fingers; a deliberate squeamishness obtains;
finally nothing is at stake. Intellectual,
is it? But why propound ideas no one would die
for or live with? The most unblinking hedonist stakes
at least his body. —Maybe what s-f needs is a
martyr, someone to risk his vanity for what he
believes an improbable truth. Then science fiction
could degenerate into religion, where they keep
imagination burning white as acetylene.

Please don't get me wrong. I'd be the last man to object
to a literature of paradigm. Borges I
love, and Aesop (quick chess pieces carved in animal
shapes), and the uncloudy delights of Sherlock Holmes, and
any story about unknown languages or codes.
It's not the skeleton that rattles me, but the flesh—
or want of it . . . And why are bureaucracies treated
as admirable or even necessary? Why
are there no devout women mentioned? Why do children
never starve or burn?

Trouble is, the difficulties
to be solved are never hard, the insolubles are
taken as premises. Thus, these novels cast themselves
away from myth, which possibly could justify them.
For myth originates then when imagination
struggles, falters, and finally takes a flying leap.
Id est, myth springs from hiatus of historical
data, a need to justify present cultural
anomaly; myth is critique of lost history.
But science fiction has no feel for pastness, and at
most a high school textbook notion of cause-and-effect;
its heroes are always blatant bloody prodigies
like Patton, Napoleon, Xerxes—*always Moloch*;
vulgar pains, almost without exception, in the ass.
Which partly accounts for s-f's garish surface (when
it has a surface), and for omnipresence of blood
(its color but not its taste). —It counts suffering out.

(Right here I want to list exceptions. Injustice to
*H. G. Wells, Olaf Stapledon, Poe, H. P. Lovecraft,*
and *Rudyard Kipling* would be ungrateful on my part.)

In my whole file of A. E. van Vogt no one changes
his socks, or chips a tooth, or shaves. No one even farms.
Those boys are always either *thinking* (something hotstuff,
you bet) or *reacting* with split-second reflexes—
like garter snakes. Not a calloused palm in a platoon
of heroes. They've got glands, all right, of the push-button
sort, but that doesn't make them human—merely in heat.
And an absence of saints: one would expect no Ghandis
or St. Claras or Schweitzers in this most secular
of literatures—but why no Curies, Oppenheims,
Galilei? These were persons; but s-f desires
merely a set of bubble-gum-card figures: the truth's
not in it, not even a lurid truth.

                    Old buddy,
here I stop bitching. No use to fault stuff that never

aimed at anything much in the first place. Probably
what troubles me most is the poets; usually
everything's their mucking, anyway. They let it get
by them, all that pure data, those images, that new
access to unplumbable reaches of space-time. They're
still whining, like flawed Dylan records, about their poor
lost innocence, and the manifold injustices
continually visited upon them, and their
purple-murky erotic lives, and their utterly
horrid forebears—maybe now and then pausing to gawk
a Flower or The Sea. The heart of it is, if the
stuff's not employed by poets, it'll find *somewhere* a
position, if it has to be among the anti-
poets. Fresh wonders clamor for language, and if the
word-order is second rate, they'll take it in lieu of
braver speech. But let me tell you, Guy, this dilemma
is a fashionable oddity left over from
the '90s (Wilde, Mallarmé, & Co.). Marvell
or Donne or Vaughan wouldn't let such opportunities
rot on the stalk; they'd already have one foot moon-bound
and a weather eye out for pulsars; they had senses
alive apart from their egos, and took delight in
every new page of Natural Theology.
(If that thought is not correct, it ought to be.) And all
this material would be virgin as an unfilled
pie shell if Heinlein and Asimov hadn't got there
first, prinking hobnail-boot tracks and scattering beer cans.

I bet you've guessed it. All these too-many pages of
flaccid syllabics are apologia for my
own absolutely magnificent science fiction
novel. Of course, it's not written yet, but I've got notes,
an outline, and fairly clear notions of what I want
to say. I hope you don't expect I'll live up to what
by negative inference my ideals seem—no one
ever does. But I'd like to make anyhow a start,

the weirder the better. Counting on your tolerance,
I append a five-stress summary.

## THE NOVEL:

Know ye, Lillian, that once upon this earth
Words had not the shape that now they shine in,
And men had earless only holes to balance
The wind that whooshed their heads, and a single eye
On the lefthand side blinked in the cheek. Strange
Beings, men of matter not of flesh,
Such creatures that walked when void and atom married;
And nothing then of the comforting mud that chinks
*Our* bones. Nor had they mouths to say or slobber.
Up and down the diamonded soil they ran,
Aimless and endless in a kind of Brownian motion.
And words lay all about the landscape, lay
Half-buried in glittering ground, or propped cockeyed
Against metallic trees . . . . For words were objects
In that crystal season, great lunking hulks
Unmanageable. Slabs of matrix unnameable,
Discrete, and silent as a birdless sky.
No one, know ye, knew what they were. The notion
Of *word* had not yet squiggled into being.
But there they were, twitchy to be discovered,
All words that in the world ever were or will.

Take "is," for example. Here was a frost-on-iron-
colored dodecahedron forty feet long
With faces unreflecting which stood at the center
Of that senseless tribal scurrying, an obstacle,
If they'd known what "obstacles" were. ("Obstacle" itself
Was a globular little pebble streaked with blue.)
Let us take "like." "Like" was everywhere,
An abrasive glinting dust bitter to taste—
Had there been mouths—cloaking all the objects

That were really words. Or think of "soul":
Small solid round cuddly boulder
You'd hug to your chest. All tongue was there:
"Tovarisch," "shantih," "amo," "Chattahoochee,"
Lying connectionless upon sterility.
No man paid them any mind.

Beyond the moon a race of beings superior
Then throve, and observed the plight of human men
With pitying hearts. *Archamens* they were called,
Of the planet *Nirvan,* which circled the deeps of Aquarius
Constellation. Flitted the galaxies
Faster than love can whisper the loins in spaceships
Constructed of intellectual soap bubbles. Knowledge
They'd gained, of the transitory and sempiternal,
And they decided to take a hand. Accordingly,
They sent an envoy, a lady who'd been awarded
Mother of the Year (on Nirvan seven
Thousand seven hundred forty days).
For her a simple task. She brought her ship
Downily to couch upon our prickly planet.
Stepped forth splendid in radiant gossamer
And took the hand of the first dumb joe who came
Along. (Later, when names came into fashion,
He spelled himself Adam.) She led him a mile
Through clanking desert to the foot of a mountain taller
Than Pisgah, hill of blue-green-gray-white flashing,
A single mineral.
                                    "Now listen to me, honey,"
She said. "I'm going to say this once, so try
To get it. What you're looking at is *water.*
You understand me? This is *water. Water.*"

Brother, you shoulda been there! Obviously,
It blew that dim ember of brain he had
To highest heat. Certainly it was water.

Why hadn't he figured it out before? *Water—*
So simple a notion . . .

And in that instant everything
Occurred that still occurs and shall occur.
From his holey head his ears began to peep
Out, tentative as snail-horns. Featureless chin
Blossomed a mouth like a red red rose, mouth
Suffering to speak. And a second eye
Bulged brightly, setting in order the face that now
We know. He struggled; sweat suffused his form.
At last he got it out. "Water," he said.
(Or maybe "wodor" or "wat-tar" or "wazzar" or "wawa.")

And the mountain itself! began to change, rumbling
Gushy, and rippling majestic as borealis,
Finally collapsing, like jello in an oven, to liquid;
And began to search the secret veins of earth.
Everything changed! Palm trees sprang forth, and lilies.
Elephants, tigers, cows, green beans, papaya . . .
Whatever name you like to name took root,
And the world filled up with glorious language, bleating
Like a million million trumpets.

Our Lovely Mother,
Satisfied (almost smirking, is my guess),
Remounted her ship and starward rode off silent.
Adam didn't even notice, so joyed
He was, so battered with delight at names
Which on every flaming side struck both his eyes.

Over and over he said it: "Water. Water."
And other words: "Pomegranate. Baseball. Mouse.
Cadillac. Poem. Paradise. Cinnamon Doughnut."
When he said, "Man," everyone changed to persons
Like himself. (Except the women, of course.)

But that one word he loved, and said again:
"Water. Water. Water. Water. Water."

## THE END

So there you have the main drift of it, at least. I'd be
curious to know what you think, so long as it is
favorable and congratulatory. If it's
not, you dog, don't even bother to answer

old Fred.

# X    On Stillpoint Hill at Midnight


The sea driving its salt wedge
into rivers,
bridges and trees plunging bare arms
into earth,
mountains through their roots
sucking earth
up to bare spaces,
and suns overhead and moons grinding
like peppermills,
and heart's-blood searching out
every tendril in the body
and returning;
each upheaval that order is,
my stillness takes in.

My stillness a method of hearing.
Elements huddling,
stars and waters sing
a whole still note.

On this hill at midnight
I, pallidly glowing
(I glow amidst the dead),
consider how the giants went
into earth
patiently to wait themselves
into stone;
considering again how stones will burgeon
into animals, erupting to four feet
on glossy lawns,
and gnawing the ruled streets and lot corners
of suburbs

like moths devouring stripes
in a bolt of plaid.

This stillness filled with potency as a pebble
flung upward, wrinkling stars in rings.

My gaze will return from sagging
fences of the stars
and once more plummet
into my eyes.
Will return battered like
an old dory
from the mole-runs of starlight
and steep cataracts
between the atoms
and once more launch into my eyes.
Appearances shall unfasten,
the world divest of illusionary bloom
loll its doped head,
flower with wounded stem.

Then shall I see you with new eyes.
We are locked like chain
steadfast,
we are fixed while around us
creation dribbles
out the bottleneck of diminishment.
We must keep calm and admire
one another now
as stones, waters, stars,
and spaces cry out
in furious concord,
heaving unceasing the unutterable
into being.

It is the wind shall cleanse us,
I tender you promise
of the wind.

All. All is moveless if only
we lie easy on the surface-
tension of history.
Remembering how
in Plemmons' springhouse with water
tunneling fast up amid mineral
crawfish, your face
white slid like a proud steam yacht
over the cold boiling-away:
so must we cohabit
with event,
touchless with our allegiances as water-
spider's feet upon stream-skin.

We will rest simple,
we will taste with our pores
the powerful probabilities massing about
indivisible infinite motes of water
as earth sweats itself
in this springhead.
Or come with me at 6 a.m.
in the woods by the lake
(carp-slap sharp as rifle shot
through ringing silence),
where I can point one drop of dew
on sassafrass leaf
which reflects the whole breadth of dawn
gray and blue-gray.
For water, like human
history, weeps
itself into being.

We must lie careless as
these forces foment,
we also must reflect every
fire of the heavens
and the cool effortless moon

trawling our faces.
Must read too the waters clouding us,
feel soup-green billows
drifting our blood, blood
prophetic with earth, wind, and star,
seas sloshing artery walls.

*Every level seeks its own water.*
*Water is whole because it is patient.*

Mostly I dare not think it:
slow rain twitching wounds and eyelids
of murdered soldiers,
daily snail-white corpses
bloating the Mekong and Hudson,
muskrat drowned chewing his leg
in the iron purse-snap,
rivers rotting to lye where
the mill-drains vomit inky venom,
current fingering endlessly jagged steel
of sunken liners
(melting the bones of the filthy rich
to gray jelly),
aborted
babies thrust into sewer pipes: how
on the sterling upper plane
of water
we the living dance thoughtless,
steady in one place,
while in the living muscle
dead men toil
and compose their strengths.
In satin inlets of our sleep
they will surface
and like pistons swim
absolutely toward us.
They depart no painted paradise

with harps and lutes
but a dread salt Sargasso
thirsting for our green blood.

The moon, Susan, 's a-tilt now.
Let us join hands, descend
this star-bathed hill
to where the study light, the kitchen
light, corridor the dark.
Let us enter breathless our leaking house,
turn bedsheets, preparing to voyage
wherever these midnight waters
stream.

We shall not fear.

We are moving still.

## XI    The River Seeks Again the Sea

Again. Deep morning.

Collect
From day, from time of stream, collect
From vagary and tic, my mind suckles your shoreless lonesomeness.
                            Susan       Susan,
Where go we now? I guess we wash towards death.
May I hold your hand?

Sometimes I look your eye to the core.
Sea I see. What promise else
Adventurous have you never?
What what what can I do burning?
We have tried our best.
We shall.

Listen, unlucky, how I see us:
The universe is bigger.
Can we belong? How do we join?
The stars come by
In tides, winds and waters peep us rancorless.
What do you wish, I wish.
No, I will also be a man.

Mind coming apart to water, searching salt springs
Of earth, or is it the sea reaching
To first fresh fingertips of water in stone in the high mountains?
What I know is, no one sleeps apart.

Ever ever
In unanimous voice we drift,
Selflessness of energies bright and blind.
We are each us. There is no me.
(I do not mind.)

The world asleep is begging us to sleep.
The world asleep
Broadens and unshapes.
What unthinkable current sweeps our grandmothers?
*We shall meet again on that other shore.*

We shall meet again, we shall meet
When now touchless my hand on your breast is swimming
Unfeeling wilderness of time present and past.
And now you mutter in dream and now you say
My dream.
Our life is gratefully asleep.

Never never
Would I wish to wake, except to kiss
Your dark eyelids febrile with dream.
Never will I wake your eyes.
The earth is shoving us to sea, the sea shoulders us
To another earth.
So we stand naked and carefree and holding

In the dew-fired earliest morning of the world.